WILDFLOWERS
OF THE OLYMPICS

100 WILDFLOWERS OF
OLYMPIC NATIONAL PARK

D0012085

By Charles Stewart

Published by

Nature Education Enterprises

P. O. Box 27103

San Francisco, California 94127

In cooperation with the

Olympic Natural History Association

Port Angeles, Washington

Introduction

This book is essentially a wildflower identification book. It is hoped that those who use this book will be able to attain a first-name acquaintance with the flowers they observe, and in doing so realize the importance of wildflowers as a bright, attractive adjunct to the somber woods, deep cleft valleys, and towering peaks and ridges of the Olympics.

Within this book are one hundred different species of wildflowers presented by color photographs and by word. Although there are over a thousand species and varieties of wildflowers in the park, the 100 pictured and described herein are among those most commonly seen. To make the identification of the wildflowers as easy as possible, the plants are grouped by color. To identify a plant look for it in its proper color section. In some instances a plant may have flowers of more than one color; if so, it is to be found in the color section of the color that most dominates. The berries of two plants are pictured rather than the flowers (#72 and #73) for the berries are more often observed and commented upon by visitors.

For each plant a text provides information that will be of interest to the observer as well as provide an aid to its identification. The text will give the approximate flowering period, but it should be emphasized that the time is only approximate. One must bear in mind that the time period during which a plant is in flower is to a large extent influenced by elevation and exposure. For example, a plant that grows at both low and high elevations may blossom in mid-July at the low elevation and not until mid-August at the high elevation. Many plants on a northern exposure or in cool, protected areas will blossom later and/or longer than those in less favorable locations. Unusually wet or dry summers can also change the flowering period. For some species you will find that the text makes note of their value as a food source. This is done only to indicate the importance that those particular plants had to early settlers and Indian tribes, and is not to be construed as an invitation to sample them. The plants of the park are protected by law, as well they should be, so that all that follow you may also enjoy their beauty. Please use care that the plants are not trampled or disturbed in any way.

In addition to the brief text, for each plant you will find grouped together for quick reference the scientific name, the family to which the plant belongs, its other common names, its distribution, habitat, and elevational zone. Particular attention should be paid to habitat and elevational zone for these two categories are very helpful in identifying plants.

DISTRIBUTION: Many of the wildflowers in this book are widespread in their distribution, so much so that the user will probably find a number of plants which are as much a part of his home area as they are a part of the Olympic scene. The general distribution of each plant is given so that the user can determine whether or not a particular wildflower can be found in his home area.

OTHER COMMON NAMES: Plants, either wild or domestic, are frequently known by several common names. The most used and acceptable common name is given for each flower. Other names by which the plant may be known are also given. Often different plants are known by the same common name, or the same plant is known by different common names, which can make the use of common names confusing at times. When in doubt one can always fall back on the scientific name for it changes little or not at all from one part of the country to the other, or, for that matter, from one part of the world to the other.

HABITAT: The kind of habitat or environment in which a plant is normally found is given. This sort of information is helpful in identifying wildflowers since many plants are highly selective in their habitats. This selectivity on the part of plants is an indication of their responsiveness to the conditions under which they live and grow. Their presence in a particular locality or habitat is the result of a combination of environmental factors to which they have become adjusted or adapted, such as temperature, moisture, wind, shade, soil conditions, and other factors. Each plant has a particular set of environmental or habitat requirements that it has acquired over a millenium of time: under the shade of trees; moist, wet, or boggy ground; the edge of streams or rivers; deep duff on forest floors; rock faces with cracks and crevices in which to send down roots for anchorage and nourishment; dry and rocky soil, or talus slopes.

Many plants have developed special structures to adapt them to a sometimes precarious but successful existence in a habitat which appears harsh and forbidding. Plants of dry, rocky areas, for example, often have thick, heavy leaves, or a light covering of "hairs" to retain water or to reduce water loss from the surface of the plant. Those plants of dense forest shade have either large, broad, flat leaves to capture every ray of light that penetrates the forest canopy, or they have no leaves at all and derive their life-giving nourishment from decaying organic matter. The fact that many plants have special structural adaptations is of importance as an aid in identification as well as adding interest to wildflower study. Look for these adaptive modifications in plant form and structure. Such modifications are noted in the text for many of the plants in this book.

ELEVATIONAL ZONE: Elevation plays a very significant role in determining what kind of wildflowers one will observe in various parts of the park. Those wildflowers that have adapted to cool summer temperatures and a short growing season will be found at higher elevations than those whose needs are for a longer growing season and higher summer temperatures. On the other hand, there are a number of highly adaptable and tolerant plants that grow successfully from low to high elevation.

Four major elevational zones are used for the purpose of this book, each with its own set of climatic and soil conditions. The zones are Lowland Forest, Montane Forest, Subalpine, and Arctic-alpine.

Lowland Forest Zone. Extending from sea level to approximately 2,000' in elevation this forest zone will be considered as two subzones: (1) the Humid Lowland Forest which is that portion of the western peninsula from Lake Crescent to the coast and south to Lake Quinault; and (2) the drier forests of the northeastern and eastern peninsula from Lake Crescent east to the Hood Canal and south to the Staircase area, which will be referred to as the Lowland Forest. The Humid Lowland Forest is dominated by Sitka Spruce, *Picea sitchensis,* Western Hemlock, *Tsuga heterophylla,* and Western Red Cedar, *Thuja plicata.* Douglas Fir, *Pseudotsuga menziesii,* and Western Hemlock characterize the drier, more easterly Lowland Forest. In the coastal portion of the peninsula there are among the forested areas open spaces or "prairies" which on the west side of the peninsula are often swampy or boggy. The prairies have sun-loving plants in contrast to the forests where the plants tolerate shade and thrive in the coolness. The areas most accessible in the Humid Lowland Forest are the Hoh Rain Forest, the Queets and Quinault Rain Forests, Mora, Lake Ozette, La Push, and Kalaloch. The Lowland Forest zone is characteristic of such areas as Heart O' the Hills, Sol Duc Hot Springs, Elwha and Altaire, Dosewallips, and Staircase.

Montane Forest Zone. A zone from approximately 2,000' to 4,000', this is the most extensive zone on the peninsula, clothing the mountain slopes with dense, virtually impenetrable forests. The more westerly mountains are dominated by Western Hemlock and Silver Fir, *Abies amabilis,* while the eastern portion has Douglas Fir, Western Hemlock, with a scattering of Western Red Cedar and Sitka Spruce. This is the realm of saprophytes, those curious plants lacking green chlorophyll and deriving their nourishment from decaying organic matter on the forest floor. Usually the Montane Forest zone is open only in fire burns, along streams, and along trails, for it is in such places that the forest canopy is broken open sufficiently to permit the penetration of enough sunlight to sustain a varied plant life. Most of this zone is accessible only by trail. However, roads leading to Hurricane Ridge, Deer Park, and Olympic Hot Springs take you into and through this zone.

Subalpine Zone. This is the highest timbered zone ranging from 4,000' to 5,800'. Typical of this zone are small to large groups of coniferous trees, the most conspicious of which are Subalpine Fir, *Abies lasiocarpa,* Mountain Hemlock, *Tsuga mertensiana,* Alaska Yellow Cedar, *Chamaecyparis nootkatensis,* and Lodgepole Pine, *Pinus contorta.* Occasional Douglas Fir and White Pine enter this zone and at this higher elevation become much stunted and deformed. Meadows are interspersed among the groups of trees; those of flat and gently sloping terrain are moist and sometimes boggy; those of steep slopes are well drained and much drier. The zone is quite similar to the subarctic regions of northern Canada. The summer temperatures are commonly cool, especially at night. The growing season is short, from the end of June to September. In this zone there is virtually a complete absence of annual plants, only the more hardy perennials can exist here. During the mid-summer period, the moist meadows and drier hillsides present the most spectacular wildflower display to be found in the park. The best time for viewing during a typical summer is the first two weeks in July. The zone is readily accessible by car at Hurricane Ridge and Deer Park.

Arctic-alpine Zone. Lying above the upper limit of tree growth this zone corresponds to the arctic areas of northern Canada and Alaska. There are many species of plants to be found in this zone that are identical with those of the far northern lands of Alaska and Canada. The zone is generally confined to the high peaks and ridges where the soil is shallow and underlain with rock. The growing season is short— mid-July to September. In some areas there is no growing season for the snow remains all summer long. The climate is rather severe for plant growth; summer temperatures are generally cool, drying winds are common which increase water loss from plants and tend to restrict their growth, even to deform them. The plants that you will find in this zone will be those that have adapted themselves to the dessicating winds, the short growing season, occasional frosty summer days and nights, low soil moisture in some areas, and instability of the ground such as loose rock and talus slopes. All plants are perennials. The only typical Arctic-alpine area that is accessible by car is Obstruction Point. A walk along either of the ridges that fan out from the end of the road to the northeast and south offer excellent examples of the plant life of this zone. Although very limited in area, the very summit of Blue Mountain, accessible via Deer Park, can be considered within this zone.

Endemic Wildflowers

Eight species of Olympic flowering plants are endemic to the peninsula, that is, they are found only in the Olympic Mountains. Why this should be so is still a matter of speculation. Botanists seem to agree that these plants are probably relicts, i.e., plants that survived the Pleistocene Ice Age. The geologic story of the Olympic Peninsula tells us that during the Pleistocene period a portion of a great continental glacier that covered most of northern North America moved down from out of what is now British Columbia, covered Vancouver Island, and piled up against the Olympic Mountains. The mountains, standing as a barrier to the southward movement of the glacier, divided the glacier, a portion moving to the west to a point beyond present-day Lake Crescent, and a portion moving east and south along what is now Hood Canal and Puget Sound. All evidence indicates that the glacier had a depth of about three thousand feet which made the peaks and ridges of the Olympic Mountains appear to float like islands in a sea of ice. The glacier effectively eliminated all plant life except the few hardy plants that struggled to survive on the higher elevations of the mountains above the level of the glacier. Eight such plants apparently still exist today, tenaciously holding their own on the high ridges and peaks of the mountains much as they did so long ago. As one would expect, all are in the Arctic-alpine zone and grow in rocky crevices or on talus slopes. The eight relicts are Olympic Rattleweed, *Astragulus cottoni;* Piper Bellflower, *Campanula piperi* (#94), White Piper Bellflower, *Campanula piperi* var. *sovereigniana;* Flett Violet, *Viola flettii* (#87); Flett Fleabane, *Erigeron flettii;* Webster's Senecio, *Senecio websteri;* Mt. Wallflower, *Erysimum arenicola* var. *arenicola;* and Rock Spirea, *Petrophytum hendersoni.*

The Olympics and Cascades

It is not surprising to find that the flora of the Olympic Mountains is quite similar to that of the Cascade Range for the two ranges lie in close proximity to one another and have somewhat similar climatic conditions. Since a large percentage of the wildflowers that grow in the Olympic Mountains also grow in the northern Cascades, most of the flowers in this book are also flowers of our sister range to the east. As a result, this book can be used profitably while in the Cascade Mountains, particularly from Mt. Rainier to the Canadian border. If a plant given herein does not grow in the northern Cascades, note is made of that in the text.

Varieties of Our Wildflowers

Sixteen of the wildflowers in this book are varieties of the species given. Because most users of this book are content to learn the common name of a wildflower and probably will have little interest in knowing the variety of a species, variety names have been excluded from the text of the flowers. However, for the more botanically and technically oriented user who might find varieties that are found in the Olympics of some value, a list of those wildflowers of varietal status is given at the end of the book.

Sources Used

Three primary sources were used to obtain some of the information given in the flower texts. The excellent five-volume series *Vascular Plants of the Pacific Northwest* by Hitchcock, Cronquist, Ownbey, and Thompson, was of inestimable value. All scientific names are taken from this work, and much of the distribution was based upon this source. An older piece of botanical literature that was particularly helpful was *A Botanical Survey of the Olympic Peninsula, Washington* by George N. Jones. One could not delve very deeply into the wildflowers of the Olympic region without sooner or later referring to a four-volume set *Illustrated Flora of the Pacific States* by Leroy Abrams and (for volume four) Roxana Ferris. All of these sources are more technical than popular, but might be of some use to the serious wildflower enthusiast. Reference was made to several papers published as a result of research by Drs. L. C. Bliss, R. W. Fonda, and R. T. Kuramoto on the plant ecology of selected areas of the Olympics. The zonation used in this book was based in part on some of their work. A short, selected bibliography is given at the end of the book and includes other references used by the author.

Acknowledgements

The author wishes to acknowledge with deep gratitude the help given to him by the Olympic Natural History Association of Olympic National Park. Especially to Mr. David Huntzinger, Chief Park Naturalist, and Mr. Robert Kaune, Park Naturalist, a word of thanks for their constant encouragement and cooperation that permitted me to compile and publish this book. The author also wishes to acknowledge the photographs contributed by others for use in this book: #70, Louie Kirk; #45, #81, #83, David Huntzinger; #30, Robert Kaune; #25, Michael Sipes; and #72, Carl Torkko. The cover photographs are by courtesy of the Olympic Natural History Association. All other photographs are by the author.

WILDFLOWERS
IN COLOR

Along the roads and trails
of Olympic National Park
the pristine beauty of lupines and larkspurs,
paintbrush and phacelia,
as well as a host of other flowers
make of the Olympics
a gallery of color
during the late spring and summer months.
It is to those who
wish more than a passing acquaintance
with the individuals
of this magnificent floral display
that this book is dedicated.

Figwort Family

Mimulus tilingi

- Larger Mt. Monkeyflower
- British Columbia and Alberta south to southern California, east to northern New Mexico.
- Along streams, in rivulets from melting snow, and other wet places where water is cold.
- Subalpine zone

ALPINE YELLOW MONKEYFLOWER ⋏ 1

These beautiful wildflowers usually are seen massed in clumps of yellow where there is cold running water or heavy surface seepage. Like many high-elevation plants, Alpine Yellow Monkeyflower is usually short, 3″ to 10″ tall, and is an early summer blossomer, bringing forth the bright yellow, tubular flowers in mid-June and brightening wet places until the latter part of July. The leaves are opposite, oval, and toothed. *Mimulus* is from *mimus* (Gr.) for a mimic, because the flowers are supposed to resemble a mask or monkey's face. The crushed leaves of some *Mimulus* were used as a healing balm for sores. Particularly noticeable along the Hurricane Ridge road as it approaches the top of the Ridge.

The yellow flowers are about 1″ across and are usually on short flower stalks that hold the flowers close to the ground. Some plants, though, may be as much as 14″ high. The leaves are of three leaflets spreading out fan-like. *Flabellifolia* means "fan-leaf," from *flabella* (L.), a fan, and *folia* (L.), a leaf. A similar Cinquefoil, that is found in the same habitat, is Varileaf Cinquefoil, *P. diversifolia,* but it has leaves of 5 to 7 leaflets that are whitish-silky beneath. Bush Cinquefoil, *P. fruticosa,* also of the subalpine zone, is shrubby with grey-green, silky-hairy leaves. Fanleaf Cinquefoil blossoms from mid-June to the end of July. Cinquefoil can easily be confused with buttercups, so compare with Subalpine Buttercup, #8.

FANLEAF CINQUEFOIL ⋎ 2

Rose Family

Potentilla flabellifolia

- Mt. Rainier Cinquefoil
- British Columbia south through Cascades and Olympics to Sierra Nevada, and in northern Rocky Mts.
- Moist meadows where sunny and warm; also along streambanks and moist talus slopes where there is ample sun.
- Subalpine zone

Sunflower Family

Eriophyllum lanatum

- Woolly Sunflower
- British Columbia south to California, east to northern Rocky Mts.
- Dry, open hillsides and roadsides, always in full sunlight.
- Montane Forest zone to Arctic-alpine zone

3 ⅄ WOOLLY ERIOPHYLLUM

From 1′ to 2′ high, Woolly Eriophyllum forms clumps which become covered with bright yellow flowers, each flower single on each of the many stems produced. The leaves and stems are woolly white, as is characteristic of so many plants that grow in dry places. The leaves are deeply lobed with lobes quite narrow. The combination of bright yellow flowers and olive-green appearance is its most recognizable features. *Eriophyllum* is from *erion* (Gr.), wool, and *phyllon* (Gr.), leaf. *Lanatum* from *lana* (L.), wool, also refers to the woolliness of the plant. Begins to blossom toward the end of July and continues to the end of August.

4 ⅃ BROADLEAF ARNICA

In this common plant a single yellow flower usually graces the end of an 8″ to 18″ stem; sometimes three flowers may arise from last leaf pair. The leaves are opposite, oval and coarsely toothed. The stem leaves are usually no more than 2 to 4 pair. Several other arnicas are found in the park, all of montane or subalpine zones, and all with paired, opposite leaves. The medicinal "arnica" that was so popular many years ago as relief for sore muscles, came from a European species. *Latifolia* means broad-leaf. Blossoms from mid-June to the end of July.

Sunflower Family

Arnica latifolia

- Mountain Arnica
- From Alaska south to Colorado and California.
- Moist, open meadows of north slopes; on warmer slopes, along streams and under or near trees.
- Subalpine zone

Sunflower Family

Agoseris glauca

- Hairy Agoseris, Mt. Daisy, Short-beaked Agoseris
- British Columbia to California and Arizona, east to Minnesota.
- Rocky soil of high mountain ridges and peaks.
- Arctic-alpine zone

PALE AGOSERIS ⋏ 5

A rugged inhabitant of heights where winters are long and the summers short. The leaves are all basal and woolly white. Only 5″ to 10″ high, the flower heads are large and entirely of ray flowers. Our plant is the variety *dasycephala* from *dasy* (Gr.) hairy, and *cephala* (Gr.) head, referring to the hairy woolliness of the receptacle holding the yellow rays. The flowers add splotches of yellow from mid-July to about the end of August. Pale Agoseris is particularly common in the Obstruction Point area.

A short, 3″ to 8″ high, succulent plant with thick, fleshy, stems and opposite leaves. The leaves are oval, ½″ or less long. The flower stalks bear at their top a group of yellow, star-like flowers with conspicuous stamens. These plants create yellow splotches of color on rocky road cuts along the Hurricane Ridge road. *Sedum* is from *sedeo* (L.) to sit, from their habit of perching on rocky ledges. Well adapted for an arid environment, yet blossoms only when sufficient water is available. Another *Sedum*, Broadleafed Stonecrop, *S. spathulifolium*, has similar flowers but has broader, paddle-shaped leaves, and is found at a lower elevation in the Montane zone. A long blossomer, Stonecrop flowers from the end of June to the beginning of August.

STONECROP ⋎ 6

Stonecrop Family

Sedum divergens

- Cascade Stonecrop
- British Columbia south in Cascade and Olympic Mts. to the Mt. Hood area of Oregon.
- Rocky places such as talus slopes, rock cliffs, rock ledges, and rocky soil, usually where it is exposed to full sunlight.
- Subalpine and Arctic-alpine zones

Mustard Family

Erysimum arenicola

- Mountain Wallflower
- Ranges south in the Cascades and Olympic Mts. to southern Oregon.
- A habitue of warm, open hillsides and ridges where the soil is well drained.
- Subalpine and Arctic-alpine zones

7 ⋏ NECKLACE ERYSIMUM

Necklace Erysimum bears many bright yellow, 4-petaled flowers grouped together at the top of its stem. The leaves are narrow, alternate, and its height is 10″ to 20″. *Arenicola* is from *areni* (L.) sand, and *cola* (L.) to dwell, from its habit of growing best in sandy, often rocky, well-drained soil. A relative of the common yellow-flowered Wild Mustard of pastures, fields, and roadsides of agricultural areas throughout the West. There are two varieties of *Erysimum* in the park, this described plant, var. *torulosum,* and var. *arenicola* which is endemic to the Olympics and an uncommon inhabitant of the highest peaks.

It is typical to find the glossy yellow flowers on this short 2″ to 6″ plant beside an ice-cold rivulet from a melting snow bank, or springing up from the cold, wet earth recently exposed by melting snow. A circle of narrow, lobed leaves are half-way up the stem. Buttercups and cinquefoils are look-alikes, but buttercups have a glossiness to the petals that cinquefoils lack; buttercups have five sepals under the petals, while cinquefoils not only have the five sepals but five small bracts between the sepals as well; buttercups require cool northern slopes or the shade of trees, the cinquefoils sunny south slopes and open fields and meadows. *Ranunculus* is from *rana* (L.) for frog, alluding to its habit of growing in wet places. Blossoms from mid-June to mid-July.

8 ⋎ SUBALPINE BUTTERCUP

Buttercup Family

Ranunculus eschscholtzii

- Snow Buttercup, Eschscholtz's Buttercup
- Alaska south to California, New Mexico and Arizona.
- Moist places in mountain meadows and on talus slopes. Usually on cool north- or east-facing slopes.
- Subalpine and Arctic-alpine zones

Violet Family

Viola glabella

- Stream Violet, Wood Violet, Yellow Violet
- Alaska south to coast ranges and Sierra-Nevada of California, east to Montana.
- Very moist situations: along streams, in seepages and boggy ground under forest trees.
- Montane forest and Subalpine zones

PIONEER VIOLET ⋏ **9**

The bright yellow "pansy-like" flowers with delicate veins of purple streaking the petals is usually readily recognized by everyone. It grows 3″ to 8″ tall and the flowers are about ¾″ across. The leaves are heart-shaped and toothed along the margin. *Viola* (L.) means violet-colored which is misleading since this flower is yellow. There are other species of *Viola* that are other than violet colored which makes the use of the name a bit confusing. *Glabella* (L.) means smooth, no doubt referring to the general texture of the plant, especially the leaves. Seeking the shade and protection of other plants, this little beauty blossoms forth from mid-June to the beginning of July.

One of the first wildflowers to appear as the snow melts away from the high alpine meadows. The graceful, pure yellow, nodding flowers give the first color to the meadows just beginning to green. Four to 12″ high, the leaves are at the base, usually two (occasionally three), and elliptical. Like its white counterpart, Avalanche Lily (#25), it often occurs in large patches. The bulbs were dried and eaten by the Indians and the leaves used as greens. *Erythronium* is from *erythros* (Gr.) red, because a species first observed by early day botanists had reddish flowers. *Grandiflorum* (L.) means large-flowered. Glacier Lily conspicuously dots the meadows of Hurricane Ridge as the snow begins to disappear. Seen at its best from mid-June to the beginning of July.

GLACIER LILY ⋎ **10**

Lily Family

Erythronium grandiflorum

- Lambstongue Fawnlily, Trout Lily, Dogtooth Violet, Snow Lily, Adder's Tongue.
- British Columbia south through mts. to northern Oregon, east to northern Rocky Mts.
- Rich, moist soil of mountain meadows, often near receding snow banks.
- Subalpine zone

Parsley Family

Lomatium martindalei

- Martindales's Lomatium
- Coastal region from British Columbia south to southern Oregon.
- Warm, dry, rocky soils where the sunlight is intense.
- Subalpine zone

11 ⋏ LOMATIUM

A mass of tiny yellow flowers top a short 2″ to 8″ stem forming a somewhat flattened, umbrella-like head. The leaves are a grey-green and are finely dissected, giving a feathery appearance. A relative, Barestem Lomatium, *L. nudicaule,* is commonly seen in the same sort of habitat—dry, rocky soils. It has similar flowers, but the leaves are not dissected, but are oval, light green, with small teeth along the edge. The seeds of Barestem Lomatium were ground by Indians and used as a medicine for consumptive ailments. The roots of a number of other species of *Lomatium* growing in the West were used by the Indians for food. Lomatium blossoms from mid-June to the end of July. Common on Hurricane Ridge, particularly along the Hurricane Hill Trail.

A shrubby plant because of the clumping of many stems arising from a woody base. Growing 10″ to 24″ tall, it bears a number of rayless white flowers that have a yellowish appearance because of protruding yellow stamens and style. The lower leaves are roundish, the upper more narrow and pointed. All leaves are alternate, green on the upper surface and white below because of a thick, hairy covering. *Hypoleuca* is from *hypo* (Gr.) below or under, and *leuca* (Gr.) white. The matted "hairs" on the under surface of the leaves prevents the loss of precious moisture from tiny, invisible openings that dot the undersurface. Blossoms from beginning of July to mid-August.

12 ⋎ LITTLE-LEAF LUINA

Sunflower Family

Luina hypoleuca

- Whiteleaf Luina
- British Columbia south to coast ranges of central California, from Cascades westward.
- Usually growing in rocky soil, in rock crevices, or on talus slopes.
- Subalpine zone

Rose Family

Luetkea pectinata

- Alaska Spirea, Luetkea, Meadow Spirea
- Alaska south in Cascades and Olympics to northern California, and south in Rocky Mts. to Montana.
- Moist, semi-shaded places, near Subalpine Fir, and in moist, open meadows.
- Subalpine and Arctic-alpine zones

PARTRIDGEFOOT ⋏ 13

A short plant, 3″ to 6″ high, with many small, yellowish-white flowers clustered at top of a single stem. Most of the leaves are basal, clustered, small, bright green, and characteristically cleft, giving the appearance of a bird's foot. Sometimes these delightful plants are often so numerous that they will form a mat. Such mats tend to protect the soil from erosion and affords a haven for a multitude of small organisms that take up residence among the matted stems. *Luetkea* is from the name of an early day Russian arctic explorer; *pectinata* is from *pectin* (L.) a comb, no doubt referring to the comb-like form of the leaves. Although they bud out as early as the end of June, the blossoming period is normally from mid-July to mid-August.

Most often growing in a rather inhospitable environment, the whitish, bell-like flowers of Alumroot are clustered along a 6″ to 8″ stem, 9 to 12 flowers per stem. The leaves are basal and on the stem, roundish, lighter green beneath, with short stiff hairs on upper and lower surfaces. The roots have an astringent, alum-like taste. Blossoms early July at lowest levels of Arctic-alpine zone to mid-August at the higher elevations. Common at Obstruction Point and summit of Hurricane Hill and Blue Mountain.

ALUMROOT ⋎ 14

Saxifrage Family

Elmera racemosa

- Elmera
- Ranges through the mountains of western Washington.
- Talus slopes, rocky ledges, and rock crevices, usually on cool north- and northwest-facing slopes.
- Arctic-alpine zone

Heath Family

Rhododendron albiflorum

- Whiteflowered Rhododendron
- British Columbia south to Oregon, east to western Montana.
- Along streams and on cool north- and west-facing slopes, often in the shelter of Subalpine Fir and Mt. Hemlock.
- Subalpine zone

15 ⋏ CASCADES AZALEA

A shrub growing to a height of 5', Cascades Azalea will sometimes become covered with white blossoms that have a yellowish tinge during the month of July. The 1" to 1½" blossoms are single or 2 or 3 blossoms together. The leaves are yellowish-green, leathery with a waxy sheen on the upper surface, and are in whorls of 5 to 7. Indians boiled the buds as a cold or sore-throat remedy. *Rhodo* (Gr.) means a rose, and *dendron* (Gr.) a tree, *albi* (L.) white and *florum* (L.) a flower, so it is literally a "white flowered tree rose." These shrubs are often bent flat by the weight of winter's snow, but firmly anchored to the ground, the shrubs prevent the snow from sliding or avalanching down the slope, thus assurring itself of an adequate supply of water as the snow melts. Relieved of the snow's weight, it quickly springs back to its normal height.

Sylvan Goatsbeard is a shrub 3' to 7' tall that bears long plumes of creamy white flowers, the individual flowers tiny and numerous. The likeness of the plume of flowers to a goatsbeard is responsible for the scientific name; *Aruncus* (L.) a goat's beard, and *sylvester* (L.) of the woods or forest. The roots of Goatsbeard were used by some Indians, after being boiled and pounded, as a tonic drink. The root pulp was used on sores. The large leaves are divided into many toothed leaflets opposite one another. This leaf characteristic separates Goatsbeard from another common plumed shrub, Creambush Spirea, *Holodiscus discolor,* which has simple, single leaves. Goatsbeard begins to blossom by mid-June; Creambush blossoms later, usually from mid-July into August.

16 ⋎ SYLVAN GOATSBEARD

Rose Family

Aruncus sylvester

- Goatsbeard
- Alaska south to northwest California, generally along the coast west of the Cascades.
- Moist wooded areas and along streams.
- Lowland and Montane Forest zones

Lily Family

Veratrum viride

- Corn Lily, Indian Poke, Swamp Hellebore
- Alaska south to Oregon, east to Rocky Mts., through Canada to Quebec, south to N. Carolina.
- Wet meadows, swampy areas, along streams where boggy.
- Subalpine zone

During early growth Falsehellebore looks much like a corn plant. The large, long, broad leaves have prominent parallel veins. Two to 4' tall, the greenish-yellow flowers are in a mass at the top of the stalk. The roots and young shoots contain a strong alkaloid poison that can be fatal to animals. The poison acts chiefly on the heart and nervous system. Unlikely to be eaten because of bitter taste. Blossoms end of July. Sometimes confused with another bog-loving plant, Yellowskunk Cabbage, *Lysichetum americanum,* whose huge, deep-green leaves are seen by trail walkers in the Lowland and Montane Forest zones.

AMERICAN ⋏ **17**
FALSEHELLEBORE

This member of the Madder Family grows to variable length, sometimes to 5' long, often trailing along the ground. The flowers are tiny, greenish-white, and in groups of three at the top of the stem. The leaves are in whorls, usually six, somewhat narrow to elliptical. The stems are square. The Lummi Indians rubbed their bodies with the plant for its good smell; the Quinnault, Klallam, and Makah Indians would mash the whole plant and put it in their hair. *Galium* is a Greek word meaning bedstraw, and *triflorum* means three flowered. Blossoms in July.

SWEETSCENTED BEDSTRAW ⋎ **18**

Madder Family

Galium triflorum

- Fragrant Bedstraw, Cleavers
- Widespread over North America, south to Mexico and Florida.
- In moist wooded areas, usually near streams or seepages.
- Lowland and Montane Forest zones

Sunflower Family

Anaphalis margaritacea

- Indian Tobacco
- Widespread over most of U.S. Throughout western states to Arizona and southern California.
- Generally where sunny and soil is dry. Common in Subalpine Fir-Alaska Yellow Cedar subalpine meadow community.
- Lowland Forest to Subalpine zone

19 ⋏ COMMON PEARLY EVERLASTING

Pearly Everlasting is often bushy, 2′ to 2½′ tall, and greyish-green in appearance. The leaves are woolly, alternate, and quite narrow. The "flowers" are white and papery; the true flowers are the yellow centers which are surrounded by white parchment-like scales. It is the presence of the long-enduring scales that gives the flower the reputation of appearing fresh and normal for long periods of time, hence the common name Everlasting. The woolliness of the leaves and stems and the reduced leaf surface are adaptations for conserving water. The Quileute Indians are reported to have used the entire plant in a steam bath to cure rheumatism. Blossoms from mid-July to the end of August.

The large, showy flowers with their white petal-like sepals brighten alpine slopes as the snow recedes. The leaves are very finely divided and soft. The stem is covered with fine hairs. Upon seeding the eye-catching flower changes into an even more striking greenish-yellow to greyish silky tassel, its long filaments drooping like an inverted mop. The flowers appear from the end of June to early July; the tassels are evident from the end of July to early August. To be seen along the road to Obstruction Point on wet hillsides.

20 ⋎ WESTERN PASQUEFLOWER

Buttercup Family

Anemone occidentalis

- Western Anemone, Tow-head Baby
- British Columbia south to Sierra-Nevada Mts., east to Idaho and Montana.
- Mountain meadows and slopes where moisture is plentiful, often at edges of snowbanks.
- Subalpine zone

Buttercup Family

Caltha leptosepala

- Marsh Marigold, Meadowbright, Heartleaved Caltha
- Alaska south through British Columbia and Alberta to Colorado, Utah, northeast Nevada and Oregon.
- Wet, marshy places, usually on cool north and northeast slopes.
- Subalpine and Arctic-alpine zones.

ELKSLIP MARIGOLD ↑ 21

The "petals" of this attractive flower are actually sepals, about 1″ long, and somewhat bluish on the underside. Stamens form the yellow center. The leaves are a light, waxy green, often folded or twisted. Growing 4″ to 10″ high, the stems are thick, reddish, and bear a single flower. Two other plants whose flowers are almost indistinguishable from Elkslip Marigold, and are found in the same wet habitat, are Twinflower Marshmarigold (*C. biflora*) and Globeflower (*Trollius laxus*). Twinflower has two flowers per stem instead of one, and Globeflower has leaves that are deeply notched and toothed along the edges. *Caltha* is Latin for marigold, and *lepto* (L.) means slender, *sepala* (L.) sepals. Blossoms from end of June to the end of July.

A common and easily recognized flower of open meadows in the Olympics. The mass of tiny, white (sometimes pinkish) flowers are borne in an oval form at the summit of a usually bare stem. The leaves are mostly at the base of the jointed stem. The roots are eaten by bears and rodents, the foliage by deer and elk, and the flowers and seed by grouse. The roots are said to have astringent and tonic properties. *Polygonum* is from *polus* (Gr.) many, and *gonus* (Gr.) an angle or joint, referring to the jointed stems. Abundant in the meadows of Hurricane Ridge and summit of Hurricane Hill. Bistort blossoms from end of June or beginning of July to beginning of August.

AMERICAN BISTORT ↓ 22

Buckwheat Family

Polygonum bistortoides

- Mt. Meadow Buckwheat, Snakeweed, Mt. Dock, Mt. Meadow Knotweed
- British Columbia south to southern California, east to Montana and New Mexico.
- Mostly in open meadows on warm south slopes.
- Subalpine zone

Parsley Family

Heracleum lanatum

- Cow-cabbage
- Alaska east to Atlantic, south over most of U.S.
- Along streams and in moist, open areas of woods.
- Lowland Forest to Subalpine zone

23 ⋏ COMMON COWPARSNIP

A large, prominent plant with massive, three-parted leaves and small, white flowers in umbrella-like groups, sometimes almost a foot across. The young stems, flowers, and roots were cooked and eaten. Some Indians burned the lower stalk and used the ashes as a salt substitute, or cooked the dry, hollow, basal part of the plant with food to be seasoned. Although not poisonous, it is similar to some species that are very poisonous, notably Poison Hemlock, *Conium maculatum,* which is widely established over North America, but absent from the park. The genus refers to Hercules, the mythical Greek strongman, because of the plant's massiveness; *lanatum* (L.) means woolly, because the stems are covered with fine, silky hairs. Blossoms from end of June through July.

24 ⋎ COMMON YARROW

A combination of finely dissected, grey-green, "feathery" leaves and small, white flowers with tiny yellow centers clustered in umbrella-like groups marks this common plant. It grows 1′ to 2′ tall. The leaves when crushed have a pungent odor. Of medicinal importance to Indians who boiled roots or leaves to use as a tea or as a poultice for skin rash or sores. The Greek god Achilles is said to have used the plant medicinally, hence the generic name Achillea. It is reported to have been used as a substitute for hops in making beer. A long blossomer, the flowers appear in early July and last until August.

Sunflower Family

Achillea millefolium

- Common Milfoil
- Widespread over northern North America.
- A wide-ranging, highly adaptable plant found in a variety of dry habitats.
- Lowland Forest to Subalpine zone

Lily Family

Erythronium montanum

- Avalanche Fawnlily,
  Alpine Fawnlily,
  Deer's Tongue
- From the Olympics,
  Vancouver Island, and
  north Cascades, south
  to northern Oregon.
- Meadows and moist,
  open places among
  trees.
- Subalpine zone

AVALANCHE LILY ⋏ **25**

One of the most strikingly beautiful wildflowers in the Olympics. The large, white, star-like flowers of Avalanche Lily, with their yellow centers, point outward rather than nodding. The leaves, usually two, are basal, elliptical, and a bright glossy green. Starting in mid-June the flowers begin to spill over meadows and among the Subalpine Fir, sometimes massed in a sea of white and yellow. As their blossoming period nears its end, around the latter part of July, the flowers turn a soft lavendar, a fitting farewell color for one of the most delightful of mountain meadow wildflowers. Most readily seen in the moist meadows of Hurricane Ridge and along the road to Obstruction Point.

The dainty, white, star-shaped flowers with their grass-like leaves are a common sight on dry, high elevation slopes in the early part of summer. Sandwort is only 4″ to 8″ high; its leaves are mostly basal, bearing only a few stem leaves that are narrow and opposite one another. *Arenaria* is derived from the Latin *Arena* for sand, because of the tendency of these plants to grow in loose, sandy soil. *Capillaris* from *capilla* (L.) hair, refers to the very narrow leaves, another example of reduced leaf surface to better adapt plant to its dry habitat.

FESCUE SANDWORT ⋎ **26**

Pink Family

Arenaria capillaris

- Mountain Sandwort,
  Rock Sandwort
- Alaska south to northern
  Oregon, east to Montana
  and Nevada.
- Most often on warm
  south and east slopes
  where soil is well-
  drained and rocky.
- Subalpine and Arctic-
  alpine zones

Lily Family

Clintonia uniflora

- Alpine Beauty, Bride's Bonnet
- Alaska south to California, east to Montana, Idaho, and eastern Oregon.
- In filtered sun of forests, usually where moist.
- Lowland, Humid Lowland, and Montane Forest zones

27 ⋏ QUEENCUP BEADLILY

An easily recognized plant because of its two (or sometimes 3) oval to lance-like leaves, 4″ to 8″ long, and a deep, glossy green. Arising on a slender stem from the center of the leaf bases is a single, pure white flower. What appear to be the petals are in reality the sepals. The flower is later replaced by the fruit, a single berry that is a strikingly beautiful blue color. Between the bright white flower and the glossy blue, bead-like berry, Queencup Beadlily is truly a forest queen. Indians, no doubt, were struck by its beauty, but they also found the plant to have some medicinal properties, for it was crushed and the juice applied to cuts or to sore eyes. Blossoms from mid-June to mid-July.

There is no mistaking this plant because of its two (sometimes 1 or 3) heart-shaped, waxy-green leaves well spaced from one another, the upper leaf smaller than the lower. At the summit of the single stem are clustered numerous small, white flowers. The flowers, late in the summer, give way to a green berry with reddish spotting (or it may be entirely red). The berries have a bittersweet taste and act as a cathartic. It is often found in association with Queencup Beadlily since it prefers the same type of habitat. *Maianthemum* is from *mai* (Gr.) the goddess to whom the month of May was dedicated, and *anthemon* (Gr.) a flower. *Dilatatum* means expanded. In blossom from mid-June to the end of July, the latter time at the higher elevations.

28 ⋎ BEADRUBY

Lily Family

Maianthemum dilatatum

- Two-leaved Solomon's Seal, False Lily-of-the-Valley
- Alaska south through Cascades and along coast to central California, east to northern Idaho.
- Along streambanks and in moist situations in open and dense woods.
- Lowland, Humid Lowland, and Montane Forest zones

Lily Family

Smilicina stellata

- Star-flowered Solomon's Seal, Wild Lily-of-the-Valley
- Alaska south to California, east to the Atlantic coast.
- In cool, moist woods where sun filters through trees, along streambanks and in seepages.
- Lowland, Humid Lowland, and Montane Forest zones

STARRY SOLOMONPLUME ⋏ 29

The 1' to 2' stems have alternate, elliptical leaves that tend to point upward. At the end of the stem are several (5 to 15) small, white, star-like flowers. A similar plant found in the same type of habitat is Feather Solomonplume (*S. racemosa*), but it differs in that it has numerous flowers instead of a few. From the flowers, berries soon form that are greenish and striped at first, but later become a bright red. The young shoots and leaves were used as greens. *Stellata* comes from *stella* (L.) a star, referring to the shape of the flowers.

A spectacular plant when in blossom, with a single, long, erect stem, the upper part of which has numerous flowers in a very large, creamy white mass. It does not flower each year—perhaps only every 5 or 6 years. The leaves are mostly basal, wiry, and grass-like. Indians used the leaves for decoration on baskets. Fibers split from the leaves were used by California Indians for basket work. Bears supposedly have a liking for the roots. *Xerophyllum* means "dry leaves" from *xero* (Gr.), and *phyllum* (Gr.) a leaf. *Tenax* is Latin for tough or holding fast, because of the tenacity with which it holds to the ground. Blossoms in July and into August.

COMMON BEARGRASS ⋎ 30

Lily Family

Xerophyllum tenax

- Turkey-beard, Squaw Grass, Basket Grass, Bear Lily
- British Columbia south to California, east to Rocky Mts. of Idaho and Montana.
- Openings in forests, open hillsides, edges of lakes.
- Subalpine, occasionally Humid Lowland and Montane Forest zones

Orchid Family

Habenaria dilatata

- Bog-candle, Leafy White Orchid
- Alaska south to California and New Mexico, east through Canada to Pennsylvania and New York.
- Wet, boggy ground along streams and in meadows.
- Montane and Subalpine zones

Clustered along the upper half of a single stalk are many sweet-scented, spurred, waxy white flowers. Close inspection reveals the flowers to be exquisitely orchid-like in form. The leaves are alternate, narrow, up to 6″ long, bright green, and clasping the stem. Growing from 8″ to 2′ tall, Bog-orchid reminds one of a candle embedded in the wet earth. The tubers were eaten by some western Indian tribes. There are four other species of *Habenaria* in the Olympics, differing primarily in the shape of the flower. White Bog-orchid blossoms during July at low elevations to August at the higher elevations.

31 ʌ WHITE BOG-ORCHID

32 ᴠ TREFOIL FOAMFLOWER

A common sight in the moist woods, this lacy, 1′ to 2½′ high plant has leaves that are divided into three leaflets, each with toothed margin; most are at base, a few along flower stalk. The flowers are many, tiny, star-like, and nodding. The Quileute Indians chewed the leaves as a cough medicine. *Tiarella* is from *tiara* (Gr.) a headdress, and *ella* (L.) small, no doubt referring to the crown of dainty white flowers. *Trifoliata* refers to the three parted leaves. Blossoms mid-June to as late as mid-August at the higher elevations.

Saxifrage Family

Tiarella trifoliata

- Three-leaved Coolwort, Laceflower
- Alaska south to northern Oregon, in Rocky Mts. from Idaho north.
- Moist forested areas, especially on moss-covered logs.
- Lowland, Humid Lowland, and Montane Forest zones

Heath Family

Cassiope mertensiana

- Merten's Cassiope, Merten's Heather, White Moss Heather
- Alaska to California and Nevada; along Canadian Rockies to Montana.
- High elevations in open areas where cool and moist.
- Subalpine zone

WHITE HEATHER ↑ **33**

A low growing, shrubby plant becoming matted at times. The leaves are tiny, only ⅛″ long, scalelike, and overlapping. The white, bell-like blossoms sometimes completely cover the shrub. Often growing with Red Mountain Heath (#65), whose pink-red flowers complement the white of Heather, making the color combination a delight to behold. In Greek legend, Cassiope, the mother of Andromeda, was so beautiful that she was lifted to heaven to become a constellation in the night sky. The sky-high mountain ridges are an appropriate place for this beautiful shrub. Because of its high elevation habitat, it blossoms late in the summer, usually from the end of July through August.

A clump of waxy white stems emerge from the duff of the forest floor to produce a single, nodding, bell-like flower on each stem. This 6″ to 10″ high saprophyte, like others common to the forest duff, derives its nourishment from decaying organic matter. It has no chlorophyll so cannot manufacture its own nourishment. Its leaves are small, alternate, white like the rest of the plant, and pressed close to the stem. As it ages it will turn black. *Monotropa* is from *mono* (Gr.) single and *trop* (Gr.) turn or change, referring to the single flower pointing in one direction. *Uniflora* means "one flower." It blossoms during the month of July.

INDIANPIPE ↓ **34**

Heath Family

Monotropa uniflora

- Singleflowered Indianpipe
- Widespread from Alaska to northern California, east to the Atlantic coast.
- Deep, shaded woods where duff on forest floor is thick and well decayed.
- Lowland and Montane Forest zones

Heath Family

Pyrola uniflora

- One-flowered Winter-green
- Alaska south to California, east to the Rocky Mts., also in eastern North America from Pennsylvania north.
- Moist, mossy places under trees.
- Montane Forest zone

35 ⋏ WOODNYMPH

One must have a sharp eye to find this mite of a plant, dwarfed by the forest trees under which it grows. Woodnymph is usually only 2″ to 3″ high, the single stem crowned by a single, white flower. The leaves are a deep green, oval, with small teeth along the margin; they are mostly at the base of the flower stalk. Woodnymph is only one of several species of *Pyrola* that are found in the park, but it is the only one bearing a single flower—the others have multiple flowers. It blossoms during July.

The white flowers form clusters that tend to roll downward and inward. The stamens extend beyond the flower and give a spider-web quality to the flower mass. The flowers quickly turn brown with age, so that often a plant will have both white and brown flowers. The leaves are cleft at the base to form one or two small leaflets. The stems and leaves are covered with small hairs. The scientific name means a "woodland bundle" from *phacelos* (Gr.) for a bundle or cluster, and *nemoral* (L.) a grove or woodland. A roadside plant along the upper part of the Hurricane Ridge road and along the Obstruction Point road. Blossoms during the month of July.

36 ⋎ WHITE PHACELIA

Waterleaf Family

Phacelia nemoralis

- Shaded Phacelia
- Along coast from Washington to central California.
- In a variety of habitats, but usually in open areas among trees, or near trees in shaded places.
- Lowland, Humid Lowland Forest zones to Subalpine zone

Rose Family

Rubus parviflorus

- White-flowering Raspberry
- Alaska south to southern California, east to the Great Lakes, south to New Mexico.
- A variety of habitats; open woods, streamsides, moist slopes.
- Lowland, Humid Lowland Forest zones to Subalpine zone

WESTERN THIMBLEBERRY ⋏ 37

This widely distributed and adaptable shrub is easily recognized by its large, "maple-like" leaves, with five toothed lobes. The large leaves, held by strong, flexible stems, adapt it well for growing in partly shaded places, for there is ample surface area to catch a maximum of light so essential to the life of a plant. Two to 8′ tall, it bears white, 5-petaled flowers that later become a red, raspberry-like, edible berry. Other parts of the shrub were used by various Indian tribes; the bark boiled and used as a soap, the young shoots eaten, the leaves boiled in the fall months to make tea. *Rubus* (L.) for a kind of berry, and *parviflorus* (L.) means "small-flowered." Blossoms from early June to mid-July at low elevations, to mid-August at higher elevations.

Dwarf Bramble trails along the ground by long stems from which come the white, five-petaled flowers and the three- to five-lobed leaves; the leaves have small teeth along the margin. It can be confused with Trailing Rubus, *R. pedatus,* which has leaves that consist of 3 to 5 separate leaflets. A third trailside plant that is somewhat similar, and found in the Lowland and Humid Lowland Forest zones, is Trailing Blackberry, *R. ursinus,* which has three leaflets with prickles, and small thorns on the stems. The fruit of Dwarf Bramble is a small, edible, dark red raspberry, *Rubus* (L.) means a bramble or berry, *lasio* (Gr.) shaggy or hairy, and *coccus* (Gr.) a berry. Blossoms from mid-July to mid- or late August, the berries usually appearing in September.

DWARF BRAMBLE ⋎ 38

Rose Family

Rubus lasiococcus

- Hairy-fruited Dwarf Bramble
- British Columbia south in Olympic Mts. and through Cascades to northern California.
- A trailside plant usually in open to shaded areas under trees.
- Montane Forest and Subalpine zones

Rose Family

Amelanchier alnifolia

- Juneberry, Shadbush
- Southern Alaska south to California, east over most of western part of U.S.
- Usually along streams, but also in moist, open woods and open hillsides.
- Subalpine zone

39 ⋏ SASKATOON SERVICEBERRY

A low shrub with oval leaves that are saw-toothed along the upper edge. The flowers are white with petals that are narrow and spaced well apart. The flowers later become black (sometimes red), somewhat mealy but sweet, edible berries. A staple in the diet of many Indian tribes of the West, they were eaten fresh or dried for winter use. Many animals find the berries, as well as other parts of the plant, to their liking. *Alnifolia* means "alder-leaved" because of the similarity of its leaves to those of the Alder. The blossoms appear about the end of June and continue into July.

Growing singly or in compact masses, Bunchberry Dogwood is an attractive element in the somber woods. The flowers of this common woodland plant are unusual for they consist of four petal-like bracts with the true flowers as greenish-yellow structures in the center. This is also characteristic of the Dogwood tree, a close relative. The whorled leaves are 2″ to 3″ long and a light green. The fruit is a cluster of bright red berries that are not edible because of their unpalatable taste. *Cornus* (L.) for horn, referring to the horny or hardwood, *canadensis* for Canada. Blossoms from mid-June to mid-July.

40 ⋎ BUNCHBERRY DOGWOOD

Dogwood Family

Cornus canadensis

- Dwarf Cornel, Crackerberry, Pigeon Berry
- Alaska south to mountains of California, east to Rocky Mts., then along northern tier of states and Canada to the Atlantic.
- Moist woods, often with Salal and ferns.
- Lowland, Humid Lowland and Montane Forest zones

Barberry Family

Achlys triphylla

- May leaves, Sweet-After-Death
- British Columbia south along coast to northwest California.
- Deep woods and open, forested areas where moist.
- Lowland, Humid Lowland, and Montane Forest zones

Although the three large, fan-like leaves are the most conspicuous part of Vanillaleaf, the flowers emerging from the center of the leaves cannot escape notice. They are small, white, and in an elongated cluster at the top of the stem. The dried leaves of this 8"- to 18"-tall plant have a faint vanilla odor. The boiled leaves were used by some Indians as a relief for tuberculosis. Its scientific name is quite appropriate for *Achlys* is Greek for gloom; *tri* (L.) is three, and *phylla* (Gr.) leaves, referring to its form and deep woods habitat. Blossoms during June, to early July at higher elevations.

DEERFOOT
VANILLALEAF ⋏ **41**

The most recognizable aspect of Adenocaulon is the triangular leaves, the upper surface of which is bright green, the under surface covered with short, whitish hairs giving a silvery appearance. When bent over the silvery undersurface mark the path of errant footsteps. One to 3' tall, the upper end of the long stem produces a tuft-like group of small, white flowers. The flowers are later transformed into small, sticky seeds that easily catch in one's clothing or the fur of an animal. *Adeno* (Gr.) a gland, and *caulo* (Gr.) a stem or stalk, referring to the somewhat sticky, glandular flower stalks. Blossoms July to beginning of August.

Sunflower Family

Adenocaulon bicolor

- Pathfinder, Silver-green, Trail Plant
- British Columbia south to California, east through Idaho and Montana to northern Michigan.
- Moist, shaded situations in forests.
- Lowland, Humid Lowland, and Montane Forest zones

AMERICAN
ADENOCAULON ⋎ **42**

Saxifrage Family

Saxifraga caespitosa

- Californian Saxifrage
- Alaska south through Cascade, Olympic, and Rocky Mts. to Oregon, New Mexico, and Arizona.
- Rocky locations such as in crevices of rock faces, talus slopes.
- Arctic-alpine zone

43 ⋏ TUFTED SAXIFRAGE

Tufted Saxifrage is a matted plant, growing only 3″ to 4″ high, the slender stems holding up delicate, white, star-shaped flowers. The leaves are its most distinguishing characteristic; mostly basal, massed in somewhat circular groups, overlapping one another. Each leaf is lobed into a "three-finger" form, the surface hairy, and the leaf succulent. *Saxifraga* is from *saxi* (L.) a rock and *fraga* (L.) to break, indicating its affinity for rock crevices. *Caespitosa* is derived from *caespit* (L.) turf or sod, and *osa* (L.) full of, referring to its matted appearance. *Saxifraga* also refers to the ancient belief that the saxifrages were beneficial in breaking up gall-stones and kidney stones. Blossoms about the middle of July to mid-August.

This sweet-scented Valerian bears its cluster of small, white flowers at the end of a long, 2′ to 3′ stem. Sometimes in open meadows, lacking the protection of trees, it may be only 6″ to 10″ tall. The opposite leaves are of three to five coarsely toothed leaflets. *Valeriana* is named after Valerian or Valerianus (L.), a Roman emperor, ruling from 253 to 260 A.D., who is said to have used a European species of valerian as a medicine. The European valerian possesses a drug that acts as a mild stimulant. Blossoms during the month of July to early August.

44 ⋎ SITKA VALERIAN

Valerian Family

Valeriana sitchensis

- Mountain Valerian, Wild Heliotrope
- Southern Alaska south to Montana, Idaho, and northern California.
- Cool, moist places under trees; sometimes in moist meadows.
- Subalpine zone

Lily Family

Streptopus amplexifolius

- Twisted Stalk, White Mandarin, Liverberry
- Alaska to California, eastward to the Atlantic coast.
- Grows in moist or wet soil, usually along streams in forests.
- Lowland, Humid Lowland Forest and Montane Forest zones

CLASPLEAF TWISTEDSTALK ⋏ 45

The light green, alternate, oval leaves wrap their bases partly around the stem. The white flowers, with their petals-sepals curved upward, hang pendant, usually one per stem or stalk. The most curious characteristic is the twist or kink in the stalk of each flower. Rosy Twistedstalk, *S. roseus,* is quite similar, but the flowers lack the kink in the stalk, and the pendant flowers are white to greenish yellow, often with a tinge of rose. The fruit of Claspleaf Twistedstalk is a bright red berry, eaten by some Indian tribes. *Streptopus* is from *strepto* (Gr.) bent or twisted, and *pus* (Gr.) a foot, describing the bent flower stalk. Blossoms in June to mid-July at the higher elevations.

A "daisy-like" flower with white ray flowers and center of yellow disk flowers. Grows most often in clumps about a foot or more in height. The leaves are many, lack petioles, and are narrow. Considered endemic to the Olympics, except for those on southern Vancouver Island. *Aster* is from the Greek *Aster* for a star, *pauci* (L.) few, and *capit* (L.) a head, all of which refers to the fact that although the plant may have many stems coming from a common root area, each stem has just a few flowers. Blossoms about mid-July and will show its bright white flowers until late August.

OLYMPIC ASTER ⋎ 46

Sunflower Family

Aster paucicapitatus

- Olympic White-rayed Aster
- Olympic Mts. and at south end of Vancouver Island. Not in the Cascade Mts.
- Warm, open slopes that are well drained and receive sun most of the day.
- Subalpine zone

Sunflower Family

Chrysanthemum leucanthemum

- White Weed, Marguarite
- A native of Europe and Asia, it has been introduced into and naturalized over much of temperate North America.
- A garden escape that is now in open fields, roadsides, and waste places.
- Lowland Forest zone

47 ⋏ FIELD OXEYEDAISY

This habitue of meadows, pastures, hayfields, and roadsides is easily recognized by its conspicuous "daisy-like" white flower with the yellow center. The flower is about 2″ across and is held aloft by a long, slim, 2′ to 4′ stem. Although a weed to farmers, it is considered a thing of beauty to the traveler who often sees them massed along the roads of the peninsula. It is the state flower of North Carolina. The Quileute Indians dried the flowers and stems, boiled them, and used the water for chapped hands. Young leaves made a palatable salad for some, but for others the odor was too strong. Blossoms from mid-June to the end of July, a few hanging on until the beginning of August.

A shrubby plant, 1′ to 6′ in height, with oval, dull green, leathery leaves whose margins are finely toothed. The urn-shaped flowers hang pendant from the stem, white with some pink, later to become dark purple to blue-black berries. The edible berries were often dried in the sun, wind, or before fires, to be eaten later at leisure. Many northern Indian tribes cooked the berries with grease, shaped them into cakes to be stored. The Makah Indians dried and pulverized the leaves for use as smoking tobacco. The common name, used wherever the plant grows, is from an Oregon Indian word for the plant. Blossoms the beginning of July, the fruit forming the latter part of the month.

48 ⋎ SALAL

Heath Family

Gaultheria shallon

- None
- British Columbia south through coast ranges to southern California; from lower slopes of mountains to ocean beaches.
- Open places in forests.
- Lowland and Humid Lowland Forest zones

Purslane Family

Montia sibirica

- Western Springbeauty, Candy Flower
- Alaska south through Cascades and Olympics to southern California, east to Montana and Utah.
- Moist, shaded places in open woods.
- Lowland and Humid Lowland Forest zones

SIBERIAN MONTIA ⋏ **49**

A rather succulent plant, 12″ to 18″ tall, with opposite, paired stem leaves. The basal leaves have long petioles or leaf stalks. The plant often has a straggly appearance as it sends its long, slim stems in every direction. The often numerous white flowers will frequently appear pinkish because of tiny pink veins on the petals. Some Indian tribes made a tea of this plant to use as a tonic, or rubbed the leaves and stems between the palms in cold water, then used the water as a hair tonic. Like so many plants, Siberian Montia was named after a person, in this case an Italian botanist, Monti. Blossoms from the end of June through July.

This showy little early summer plant has white flowers with slight veins of pink, the petals notched. It is a short plant, 4″ to 10″ high, with opposite, oval leaves. The plant arises from a bulb-like corm that lies well below soil level. The corms are dug up and eaten by marmots and other wildlife; the leaves are also used as food for some animals. *Claytonia* is from John Clayton, an early-day botanist; *lanceolata* refers to the lance-shaped leaves. It blossoms from mid-June to the end of July. Common in Big Meadow on Hurricane Ridge and at the summit of Hurricane Hill.

WESTERN SPRING BEAUTY ⋎ **50**

Purslane Family

Claytonia lanceolata

- Groundnut, Lanceleaf Springbeauty
- British Columbia south to southern California, east to the Rocky Mts.
- Moist meadows, the edge of rivulets and streams, and moist places under trees.
- Subalpine zone

Primrose Family

Trientalis latifolia

- Pacific Starflower, Indian Potatoes
- British Columbia south to northern Idaho and central California.
- Forests where shaded, cool, and moist. Often under overhanging shrubs.
- Lowland, Humid Lowland, and Montane Forest zones

51 ⋏ WESTERN STARFLOWER

A delicate plant with a slender, single stem at the top of which there is a whorl of five or six, pointed leaves. From the point of attachment of the leaves there arises two or three star-like, white to pinkish flowers, borne on very slender stems. The entire plant is about 4″ to 10″ tall, more often about 6″. *Trientalis* is from *trient* (L.) one third, and *alis* (L.) pertaining to, alluding to the height of the plant, approximately one-third foot. Begins to blossom toward the end of June, and can be seen until late July at the higher elevations of the zones in which it is found.

Many stems grow from the base of this plant, bearing alternate, narrow, toothed leaves. Ten to 12″ tall, the leaves and stems are reddish. A pair of white, pinkish tinged flowers are at each leaf axile. Look closely and you will see that one petal is curved and beak-like, or as some imaginative individual thought, shaped like a sickle. *Pedicularis* is from *pediculari* (L.) for a louse, named in the belief that cows had more lice after eating plants of the genus. *Racemo*sa is from *racemus* (L.) a cluster, referring to the flowers clustering at the top of the stem. Blossoms from mid-July to mid-August.

52 ⋎ SICKLETOP PEDICULARIS

Figwort Family

Pedicularis racemosa

- Leafy Lousewort, Contorted Lousewort, Parrot's-beak
- British Columbia and Alberta south to central California and New Mexico.
- Openings in and around Subalpine Fir.
- Subalpine zone

Pink Family

Silene parryi

- Campion, Wild Pink
- British Columbia south to Cascades and Olympics in Washington, east to Rocky Mts.
- Open, dry area on warm hillslopes.
- Subalpine and Arctic-alpine zones

CATCHFLY ⋏ **53**

The most conspicuous part of Catchfly is the involucre, or that part of the flower from which the five petals emerge. It is long, inflated, hairy, and very sticky. The flowers are white, but turn pink with age. The leaves are opposite, very narrow, and occur at the joints of the stem. Eight to 12″ high. *Silene* is from *silen* (Gr.) foam, or *sialon* (Gr.) saliva. It matters not which meaning is correct, for both refer to the sticky secretion of the leaves of some species, but particularly to the stickiness of the involucre of our plant with which it is suppposed to catch flies. Blossoms from mid-July to mid-August.

A spreading, ground-hugging plant with very small, clustered leaves that are light green, stiff, and pointed. The flowers are small, less than ½″ across, and are white, pink, or light lavendar. The blossoms are so numerous, at times, that they will completely hide the leaves. *Phlox* is a Greek word meaning "a flame" in reference to the brilliance of the flowers. An excellent plant for stabilizing soil on steep slopes as it is deep rooted and will spread over a wide area. It also plays an important role in holding snow on steep hillsides during the winter months. Blossoms from mid-June to the latter part of July.

SPREADING PHLOX ⋎ **54**

Phlox Family

Phlox diffusa

- Carpet Pink
- British Columbia south through mountains to Sierra-Nevada, east to Idaho and Montana.
- Open, rocky slopes and hillsides where sunlight is most intense.
- Subalpine and Arctic-alpine zones

Buttercup Family

Anemone multifida

- Windflower
- Arctic tundra of Alaska south to northern California and New Mexico, east to New York.
- Meadows where ample moisture, rivulets from melting snow.
- Subalpine zone

55 ⋏ HUDSONIAN ANEMONE

Like all anemones, this plant lacks petals; the sepals are petal-like, greenish to bluish white, and turn upward to form a cup. The leaves are much divided and hairy. It is low growing, 4″ to 10″ in height, in response to the windy, cool high country in which it is found. The variety we have in the park, *hirsuta,* is found mostly in the Olympics, only occasionally in the north Cascades. *Anemone* comes from *anemos* (Gr.) wind, for it is at home on the wind-swept mountain slopes. An early blossomer, it comes forth as the snow recedes, from mid-June to mid-July.

Although not restricted to the Olympic Mts., it is well-represented here, for the Olympics offer the type of high, timberline environment condusive to its growth. The white to pinkish flowers are grouped at the end of a 3″ to 8″ somewhat flattened stem. The narrow, fleshy, basal leaves are often curled at the tip. Do not confuse with Tapertip Onion (#74) which flowers later in the summer and whose leaves wither during or before flowering. *Crenulatum* is from *crenul* (L.) a notch, referring to the sometimes broadly notched edges or wings on the flattened flower stem. The bulbs are small and edible. Blossoms from the end of June to the end of July.

56 ⋎ OLYMPIC ONION

Lily Family

Allium crenulatum

- Notched Onion
- Spotty occurrence west of Cascades from Vancouver Island south to Oregon. Not in north Cascades.
- In dry, gravelly soils, on slopes warmed by the sun most of the day.
- Subalpine zone

Honeysuckle Family

Linnea borealis

- Western Twinflower
- Northern Canada and Alaska south to California, Arizona, and New Mexico.
- Open or dense woods where there is filtered sunlight. Often in association with Bunchberry Dogwood.
- Lowland and Montane Forest zones

LONGTUBE TWINFLOWER ⋏ 57

The delicately fragrant flowers are distinctive; pinkish, bell-shaped, and nodding in pairs, they crown the end of a 4″ to 6″ erect stem. Creeping over old stumps and forest debris, Twinflower forms prostrate groups composed of slender, woody stems, with opposite leaves that are oval, about ½″ long, bright green, and glossy. The upper margin of each leaf is slightly notched. *Linnea* is from Linnaeus, famous Swedish scientist and father of the modern system of naming plants by an orderly use of Latin and Greek words as scientific names. *Borealis* (L.) means northern, for the plant is widely distributed over the northern part of the world. Blossoms by the end of June at the lowest elevations, to as late as mid-August at its highest elevation.

A saprophyte that lacks chlorophyll, so its roots must derive nourishment from the decaying organic matter in the soil. It relies to a large extent upon the fungi that inhabit the soil and bring about decay and release of nutrient materials suitable for use by Pinedrops. The 1½′- to 3′-tall stalk is brownish and sticky. The flowers are white, bell-like, and nodding on downward curved stalks. It blossoms from bottom upward. The leaves are small, narrow, and inconspicuous. *Pterospora* is derived from *ptero* (Gr.) a wing, and *spora* (Gr.) a seed, because of the broad wing on each seed. It will make its appearance any time during the summer months.

WOODLAND PINEDROPS ⋎ 58

Heath Family

Pterospora andromedea

- Pinedrops, Giant Birdsnest
- Alaska south to southern California and New Mexico, east to Atlantic coast.
- Beneath canopy of forest trees in deep duff or humus of forest floor.
- Lowland and Montane Forest zones

Heath Family

Vaccinium membranaceum

- Mt. Bilberry, Black Mt. Huckleberry, Thinleaf Huckleberry
- British Columbia south to northern California, east to Idaho and Montana.
- Open hillsides of cool north slopes, and open forests.
- Montane Forest to Subalpine zones

59 ⋏ BIG WHORTLEBERRY

A shrubby, deciduous plant that will be 3' to 4' high at lower elevations, to only 8" high at the highest elevation. When the new leaves emerge in the late spring and early summer, they have a conspicuous reddish tinge; they are thin, oval, with fine marginal teeth. The flowers appear in July, are pinkish to reddish, bell-shaped, or urn-shaped because of united petals. The black, edible berries are ripe by late August, and are much sought after by many animals, especially black bears. In Europe similar plants that were native were called Whortleberries, but settlers in U.S. changed pronounciation to Hurtleberry, then eventually to Huckleberry. There are several other species of Huckleberries in the park, ranging from Wild Cranberry, *V. oxycoccus,* of bogs and wet prairies of the Humid Lowland Forest to the low, mat-like Delicious Huckleberry, *V. deliciosum,* of the Subalpine zone.

The nodding, pink, waxy-looking flowers of this forest plant are a pleasing contrast to the somber shadings of our forests. The leathery, evergreen leaves are in several whorls, light green beneath and darker green above, with small teeth along the margins. The 5" to 8" single stem bears a group of three to eight flowers. *Chima* (Gr.) means winter, *phila* (Gr.) loving, referring to the fact that it is evergreen. *Umbellata* (L.) refers to the umbrella-like flower arrangement. The Indians made a beverage or tonic by boiling the leaves. The leaves have an astringent quality as well. Blossoms by end of June at lower elevations to mid-August at higher elevations.

60 ⋎ COMMON PIPSISSEWA

Heath Family

Chimaphila umbellata

- Western Prince's Pine
- Alaska to southern California, east to Colorado Rockies. Also eastern U.S.
- Under conifers of drier forested areas.
- Lowland and Montane Forest zones

Fumitory Family

Dicentra formosa

- Beautiful Bleedingheart
- British Columbia to central California along coast.
- Open forests along streams, near ponds and seepages.
- Lowland, Humid Lowland, and Montane Forest zones

PACIFIC BLEEDING HEART ⋏ 61

An inhabitant of shady places where there is rich soil, this 1' to 2' high plant brightens the forest with its light pink, heart-shaped flowers. Nodding in the slightest breeze, the delicate flowers seem a fitting complement to the feathery, light green, deeply dissected, thin leaves. Many of the genus *Dicentra* possess poisonous alkaloids that can have a serious affect on grazing animals. *Dicentra* is from the Greek *di,* double, and *centra,* center, because of the two-sided form of the flower. The species name *formosa* (L.) graceful or beautiful, is appropriate. Blossoms from the end of June to mid-July.

The rose-pink flowers of Baldhip Rose are a delight to the eye as well as pleasing to the sense of smell. This low, shrubby plant bears its flowers from late June at the lower elevations to the beginning of August at higher elevations. The flowers are about 1/2" to 3/4" across, smaller than Nootka Rose (#63), with which you want to make a comparison so as not to confuse the two. The leaves are divided into five to eight toothed leaflets. There are spines on the stems, but they are weak and harmless. A weak but palatable tea can be made from the leaves, and the hips or seed pods are edible.

BALDHIP ROSE ⋎ 62

Rose Family

Rosa gymnocàrpa

- Wild Rose, Wood Rose, Dwarf Rose
- British Columbia south to California; parts of Montana and Idaho.
- Open places in forests, and along edge of more dense stands of conifers, usually where it is moist.
- Lowland, Humid Lowland Forest zones to, occasionally, Subalpine zone

Rose Family

Rosa nutkana

- Wild Rose
- Alaska south to northern California, east to Colorado and Utah.
- Open places in forests; occasionally on open hillsides where there is ample sun.
- Lowland, Humid Lowland Forest to Subalpine zone

63 ⋏ NOOTKA ROSE

The fragrant 2″-wide flowers of Nootka Rose are beautiful to behold. Sometimes solitary, occasionally one to three flowers in a cluster, the pink flowers adorn the 2′- to 5′-tall shrub. The fragrance on a warm summer day can be overwhelming. The leaves are divided into paired leaflets that are light green with toothed margins, and bear sharp prickles beneath. The hips or seed pods are edible but a little bitter. They are said to be delicious after being frozen and thawed, which seems to destroy most of the bitterness. Blossoms during July to the beginning of August. Nootka Rose differs from Baldhip Rose (#62) in the former's larger flowers and sharp spines.

A shrubby plant with a mass of small pinkish or rose-colored flowers in flat-topped clusters. The 1′ to 3′ shrub has leaves that are oval to narrow-oval, toothed along the upper half of the leaf. *Spirea* is from *spira* (L.) a spiral, coil, or wreath, referring to the form of the flower group. *Densiflora* (L.) means "thick with flowers." A close relative, Douglas Spirea (*S. douglasii*) is found in the subalpine zone, too, as well as the montane zone. Unlike the flat-topped flower clusters of Subalpine Spirea, the pink flowers of Douglas Spirea are in an elongated mass, the stamens of each flower being quite conspicuous. Subalpine Spirea blossoms in July.

64 ⋎ SUBALPINE SPIREA

Rose Family

Spirea densiflora

- Rose-colored Meadow-Sweet, Pink Meadowsweet, Mt. Spirea
- British Columbia south to northwest California and Sierra-Nevada, east to Montana and Idaho.
- Alongside streams and moist meadow edges, open slopes, or near groups of trees in otherwise open areas.
- Subalpine zone

Heath Family

Phyllodoce empetriformis

- Pink Mt. Heather, Red Heather, Mt. Heath
- Alaska south to California, east to Idaho and Montana.
- Open hillsides on cooler north- and east-facing slopes, or in warmer sites under or at edge of subalpine trees.
- Subalpine zone

A low-growing, spreading, matted plant with deep green, needle-like leaves. The flowers are many, small, bell-shaped, and nodding. Red Mountainheath is an evergreen that sends its roots deep into the soil to hold firmly and tenaciously despite the weight of winters snow; it is one of the many shrubs that holds the snow on steep hillsides. *Empetriformis* is from *em* (L.) in or into, *petri* (Gr.) a rock or stone, *formis* (L.) a form or shape, possibly alluding to the tenacity with which the plant holds itself to the ground. Blossoms about mid-July and will brighten many hillsides · until mid-August.

RED MOUNTAINHEATH ⋏ 65

In the high meadows during late June and early July the curious Pink Plumes can be seen with their nodding, reddish pink, bell-shaped flowers. At the summit of the short, 6″ to 8″ stem, three flowers bend downward, hanging pendant until seeding. Around the end of July each flower bends upward and is transformed into a mass of light-brown fruiting plumes from which the plant derives its name. Common in the meadows on Hurricane Hill.

PINK PLUMES ⋎ 66

Rose Family

Geum triflorum

- Grand-father's Beard, Lion's Beard, Purple Avens
- British Columbia south to California and New Mexico, east through Canada and northern U.S. to Atlantic.
- Warm, open south- and east-facing slopes and meadows.
- Subalpine and Arctic-alpine zones

Figwort Family

Digitalis purpurea

- Purple Foxglove
- Southern British Columbia to California.
- A native of Europe it was introduced into our area as a garden plant, but it escaped and is now well-established along roadsides and other disturbed areas.
- Lowland and Humid Lowland Forest zones

67 ⋏ COMMON FOXGLOVE

A tall plant, 3′ to 6′ high, Foxglove has the upper one-third of its main stem covered with drooping tubular flowers that open from bottom to top. The flowers are usually pointing in one direction. It grows most successfully in light, rich soil with full sun or partial shade. All parts of the plant contain certain glucosides which act as heart stimulants and depressants, of which digitalis is the best known. This glucoside has been important in the medical field for many years as a heart stimulant. Blossoms from the end of June to the end of July.

68 ⋎ PINESAP

A saprophyte that derives its nourishment from the decaying leaves and debris in which it grows. Eight to 10″ high, it is reddish to dull yellow with delicate, nodding flowers along the upper part of the stem. The leaves are oval, very small, and clustered along the stem. Since Pinesap cannot manufacture its own nourishment because it lacks chlorophyll, the leaves are more ornamental than functional. *Hypopitys* is from the Greek words *hypo,* under or beneath, and *pitys,* pine or fir. Blossoms from the end of June through July.

Heath Family

Hypopitys monotropa

- Indianpipe
- British Columbia south to northwestern California, east to the Atlantic coast.
- Shade of forests where deep humus covers forest floor.
- Lowland and Humid Lowland Forest zones

Lily Family

Lilium columbianum

- Small Tiger Lily, Oregon Lily
- British Columbia south to northern California, east to Idaho and Nevada.
- Open forests, dry meadows and hillsides, often in partial shade.
- Lowland Forest to Subalpine zone

COLUMBIA LILY ⋏ 69

Columbia Lily will strike many observers as familiar. It has a number of related and domesticated counterparts in gardens. This wild lily is a tall plant, 1' to 3' high, with beautiful, nodding, orange flowers, whose curved sepals and petals are covered with brownish spots. The leaves are narrow, alternate or opposite, or both, and whorled. The bulb from which this eye-catching plant arises was roasted and used as food by many Indian tribes. Fortunately, that sort of use is a thing of the past, for such a lovely plant deserves a better fate than ending in a roasting pit. Blossoms in late June at the low elevations, to mid-August at the high elevations.

As one can quickly observe, the five petals of the flower form long spurs resembling an eagle's foot, hence, the generic name, *Aquilegia*, from *aquila* (L.) an eagle. The leaves consist of three leaflets, each deeply lobed. The roots were eaten by some Indian groups; the milky root sap was used on sores to hasten healing. At the middle elevations Sitka Columbine brings forth its bright red flowers by the end of June, and will continue to blossom at the higher elevations until the beginning of August.

SITKA COLUMBINE ⋎ 70

Buttercup Family

Aquilegia formosa

- Northwest Crimson Columbine
- Southern Alaska south to northern Baja California, east to the Rocky Mts.
- Along streams, in shaded and open places where the soil is moist.
- Montane Forest and Subalpine zones

Figwort Family

Castilleja hispida

- Harsh Paintbrush, Northwestern Paintbrush
- Northwest Montana to Vancouver Island, south to Oregon.
- Open grassy meadows and hillsides in full sun.
- Lowland and Montane Forest zones to Subalpine zone

71 ⋏ HAIRY PAINTBRUSH

Like virtually all of the Paintbrushes, there is color variability in Hairy Paintbrush for, though commonly red, it can be orange or yellow. *Hispida* (L.) means hairy or bristly, referring to the conspicuous short hairs that cover stems, leaves, and colored bracts. The leaves are toothed or cleft, and this characteristic plus the hairiness of the plant set it apart from other Paintbrushes in the park. In the subalpine zone it grows 8″ to 12″ tall, but at the lower elevations it may be as much at 2′ tall. Like all Paintbrushes and related plants, the colorful part of the plant is a group of modified leaves or bracts; the actual flowers are small and hidden behind or within the bracts. Blossoms in early July to mid-August.

A conspicuous plant because of very large, maple-like leaves that are held horizontally 3′ to 8′ above the ground. The flowers are small and clustered at the top of the main stem. In late summer the flowers are replaced by a group of polished red berries. The stems and the veins of the leaves are armed with many sharp spines. The scientific name describes the plant well: *oplo* (Gr.) armor, *anax* (Gr.) a king or chief, and *horrid* (L.) rough, prickly, or to bristle. The bark was dried, pulverized and used as perfume or deodorant. The Lummi Indians made a reddish-brown face paint by mixing burned sticks from the plant with grease. The flowers appear in late May and blossom until late June. The berries are seen through most of the summer.

72 ⋎ AMERICAN DEVILSCLUB

Ginseng Family

Oplopanax horridum

- Devil's Club
- Alaska south to southern Oregon, east to Idaho and Montana.
- Along streams, in moist areas of open woods.
- Lowland, Humid Lowland, and Montane Forest zones

Honeysuckle Family

Sambucus racemosa

- Coast Red Elderberry
- Alaska south to central California, east through Canada and northern U.S. to Atlantic coast.
- Moist places in forests, along streams; common roadside shrub.
- Lowland and Humid Lowland Forest zones, occasionally Montane Forest and Subalpine zones

PACIFIC RED ELDER ⋏ **73**

Pacific Red Elder is a large shrub, 1' to 18' high, that is observed by most everyone who travels the Olympic Peninsula. Beginning in May it produces yellowish white flowers and bears them until June. The leaves are opposite and consist of five to seven leaflets, each with toothed margins and a sharp point at the tip. During July and August the flower clusters become dense clusters of small, smooth, bright red berries. The berries are not edible, and are even reputed to be poisonous. However, many Indian tribes used the berries by steaming them on hot rocks or storing them in cool water. The leaves were put on bee stings and the bark yielded a black dye. *Sambucus* means the "elder tree;" *racemosa* (L.) a cluster, referring to the berries.

One of three species of onion common to our area, Tapertip is 6" to 10" tall with a group of eight to twelve rose-purple flowers in an umbrella-like cluster. Leaves are slender, basal, and wither during or before flowering; the latter characteristic makes it easily identifiable. Like other species of *Allium* (L. for garlic or onion) the bulb is edible, either fresh or roasted. *Acumina* (L.) means a point or pointed, referring to the point on the leaves. The Indians crushed the leaves and rubbed them on the body to repel insects. Blossoms from the end of July to the beginning of August.

TAPERTIP ONION ⋎ **74**

Lily Family

Allium acuminatum

- Hook's Onion, Hooker's Onion
- Northwestern Washington, and east of Cascades to Wyoming, Colorado, Arizona, and northern California. Not in north Cascades.
- Dry, sunny, open hillsides where soil is rocky.
- Lowland and Montane Forest zones

Figwort Family

Pedicularis groenlandica

- Little Red Elephant, Elephanthead Lousewort
- British Columbia south to California, east to Rocky Mts., then through Canada to Labrador.
- Wet meadows, seepages, and near small streams.
- Subalpine zone

This is one of the most easily recognized of subalpine plants. The flowers are so unique and peculiarly formed as to be almost unbelievable. The petals have curved and elongated to assume their incredible shape. Rising to a height of 6″ to 12″, Elephanthead stands out with stately splendor in a wet meadow or water-soaked hillside. The leaves are alternate and divided; the stems often clustered in groups. *Groenlandica* means Greenland, undoubtedly because it is so at home in high, snowy places. Blossoming begins about the middle of July and ends the beginning of August.

75 ⋏ ELEPHANTHEAD PEDICULARIS

The nodding, purplish-pink flowers point their stamens groundward, the five petals curving back over the ovary. Although mostly purple-pink to pink, the petals are at times a soft lavendar. The leaves are in a circle at the base of the plant, lance-like, and about one-half as long as the plant is tall. Although Olympic Peninsula Indian tribes were not known to use Shooting Star for food, other species of *Dodecatheon* in parts of the West were used—usually the roots and occasionally the leaves. *Dodecatheon* is from the Greek words *dodeka,* twelve and *theoi,* gods. Blossoms during the month of July.

76 ⋎ JEFFREY SHOOTING STAR

Primrose Family

Dodecatheon jeffreyi

- Cowslip
- Alaska south through Cascades and Olympics to the southern Sierra-Nevada Mts. of California, east to Idaho and Montana.
- Meadows and along streams wherever soil is moist.
- Subalpine zone

Figwort Family

Mimulus lewisii

- Red Monkey-flower
- British Columbia south to California, east to the northern Rocky Mts.
- Along streams and rivulets, around springs and in seepages.
- Subalpine zone, but occasionally to Montane Forest zone

LEWIS MONKEYFLOWER ⋏ **77**

A late blossomer at high elevations, Lewis Monkeyflower brightens streamsides from the end of July to the end of August. Especially noticeable along rivulets from melting snow. Only 4″ high at subalpine elevations, it will grow to 2′ high at lower and more favorable habitats. The rose-colored, tubular flowers and opposite, oval leaves with teeth along the margin, are unmistakable characteristics. A close relative of Alpine Yellow Monkeyflower (#1) and of a third monkeyflower, Common Monkey-flower, *M. guttatus,* whose yellow blossoms are seen in July and early August at the lower elevations of the Lowland, Humid Lowland Forest, and Montane Forest zones.

The high meadows and slopes are brightened by the short, 6″ to 8″, but colorfully conspicuous Owlclover. Because of its small size, it is often overlooked by passersby. When observed one must look carefully to see that the flowers are very tiny, pink and white, and barely protrude from behind lavendar-colored bracts. Similar to Magenta Paintedcup (#88) but much shorter. *Orthocarpus* refers to the shape of the seed forming structure for it is derived from *ortho* (Gr.) straight, and *carpus* (Gr.) a fruit. *Imbricatus* (L.) means a roof tile or shingle, which refers to the bracts overlapping one another like shingles on a roof. Blossoms from mid-July to well into August.

OWLCLOVER ⋎ **78**

Figwort Family

Orthocarpus imbricatus

- Mountain Orthocarpus
- Olympic Mountains; only other location is northern California to central Oregon. Not in north Cascades.
- Open meadows and slopes where sunny and warm.
- Subalpine zone

Evening Primrose Family

Epilobium angustifolium

- Great Willow-herb, Blooming Sally
- Widespread over most of North America, Alaska to California, east to the Atlantic coast.
- Moist, rich soil of open woods and disturbed areas such as roadsides.
- Lowland Forest to Subalpine zone

Common in old fire burns and logged-over areas, the colorful massed purple-pink flowers of Fireweed tend to moderate the scarred land. Two to 5′ tall, the flowers blossom progressively upward along the stem. The leaves are narrow and lance-shaped; they are fed upon by deer and elk, but also can be used as a tea, and the shoots eaten like asparagus. Long slender seedpods will produce hundreds of seeds bearing white, fluffy tufts that carry away in the slightest breeze. Indians used the seed fluff with duck feathers in weaving blankets. Blossoms from mid-July to mid-August.

79 ⋏ FIREWEED

Splashes of pink on a hillside calls attention to this common subalpine plant, growing close to the ground, mat-like. When in flower it becomes covered with blossoms, a group of several flowers at the end of each short stem. The leaves are small, ½″ or less, and crowded at the base of the plant. Named as a commemorative to D. Douglas, an early-day botanist who explored much of the Pacific Coast in the early 1800's, studying and collecting its plants. *Laevigata* is from the Latin for smooth or slippery, which it can be if one should try to walk on it on a steep hillside. Blossoms from mid-June to mid-July.

80 ⋎ SMOOTH DOUGLASIA

Primrose Family

Douglasia laevigata

- Mountain Primrose, Cliff Douglasia
- Central Cascade and Olympic Mts. south to northwestern Oregon.
- Rock ledges and crevices, rocky soil, and talus slopes.
- Subalpine zone

Heath Family

Rhododendron macrophyllum

- California Rhododendron
- British Columbia south to northern California.
- Moist, humid forested areas, under trees where shaded and cool.
- Lowland and Humid Lowland Forest zones

COAST RHODODENDRON ↑ **81**

A 5′ to 15′ shrub whose large, showy, pinkish flower is the state flower of Washington. The leaves are elliptical in form, thick and leathery, light green above with a whitish coat on the underside. An early blossomer, the flowers enliven the roadsides and trailsides with color during May and early June. The other Rhododendron of the Peninsula is Cascades Azalea (#15) which is found at high elevations. *Rhododendron* is from *rhodo* (Gr.) a rose, and *dendron* (Gr.) a tree, literally a tree rose, although it is not a rose at all. *Macrophyllum* means "big leaf," which is certainly appropriate.

The sometimes drooping, rose-purple flower heads cluster at the top of a 2′ to 5′ stem. The leaves are deeply lobed and have sharp spines. The best way to tell it from the other two common thistles is by the woolly, weak-spined involucre. The young stalks are edible when peeled and boiled. The Chinook Indians also used the roots. Indian Thistle is our native thistle, unlike its two counterparts at lower elevation, Canada Thistle, *C. canadensis,* and Pasture Thistle, *C. vulgare.* These two thistles were introduced from Europe and are mostly roadside plants or invaders of pasture land. Pasture Thistle has a few large, purple flower heads; Canada Thistle has many small, light purple heads. Indian Thistle blossoms during July to beginning of August.

INDIAN THISTLE ↓ **82**

Sunflower Family

Cirsium edule

- Cayuse Thistle, Edible Thistle
- British Columbia south to southern Washington, from Cascades to coast.
- Moist meadows or forests; sometimes at roadsides and trailsides in dry situations.
- Montane Forest and Subalpine zones

Rose Family
Rubus spectabilis
- Yellowberry
- Alaska south to northwestern California.
- Moist situations, along streams, swampy or boggy areas, lake edges, meadow edges, and moist forests.
- Lowland and Humid Lowland Forest zones

83 ⋏ SALMONBERRY

A common shrub to 6′ in height with leaves of three doubly toothed leaflets. The stems are brown and have scattered, weak spines. The flowers of five petals are reddish-purple to pinkish-purple. They blossom in May and June. Toward the end of June and during all of July the yellow to sometimes orange or red berries form. The berries are edible but one must acquire a liking for them for their taste can be rather bland. To the Indians the bark and leaves were of some medicinal value because of their astringent qualities. *Spectabilis* is a Latin word meaning visible or remarkable.

Prunella is a corruption of a German name for a throat or jaw disease which the European form of this plant was supposed to alleviate. One Indian tribe used the juice from the crushed plant on boils and other skin infections. But it is the group of blue-purple flowers that is most striking about Selfheal. Clustered at the top of a 4″- to 10″-square stem, the individual flower is exquisitely formed and colored. The leaves are opposite, elliptical-oval, and thin. *Vulgaris* (L.) means common or commonplace. Selfheal blossoms during the month of July.

84 ⋎ COMMON SELFHEAL

Mint Family
Prunella vulgaris
- Heal-all, All Heal
- Widespread in distribution, over most of the U.S.
- Moist places, usually where soil has been disturbed such as trail edges, roadsides.
- Lowland, Humid Lowland Forest and Montane Forest zones

Figwort Family

Penstemon nemorosus

- Woodland Penstemon, Beardtongue Penstemon, Turtlehead Penstemon

- Washington south to northwestern California.

- Semi-shaded places in forests, open slopes where moist.

- Lowland Forest to Subalpine zone

GROVE PENSTEMON ⋏ **85**

This woodland penstemon has stems that tend to grow horizontally or, at times, prostrate. The large, opposite, coarsely toothed leaves are spaced along the 1′ to 2′ stem. The light blue to rose-purple flowers are grouped at the end of the stem and usually point outward. Recognition characteristics are its close association with trees, the nearly horizontal position of the stems, and the two to five flowers at the end of the stem. Altough this plant was probably not used medicinally, some penstemons were used as poultices, the leaves boiled and used for that purpose. Blossoms from mid-July to mid-August.

The light pink-purple rays of this 6″- to 16″-high plant are a common sight during the summer. The flowers are usually solitary, one per plant, with the rays numbering thirty to forty, each with a small projection or tooth at the tip. The leaves are alternate. *Erigeron* is from *eri* (Gr.) early or spring, and *geron* (Gr.) an old man, probably because of the early appearance of some species in the spring. *Peregrinus* is from *peregrin* (L.) to wander, because of its wide distribution. Fleabane means flea-poison (bane from the Old English for poison) because the plant is reputed to repel fleas. The Aster part of the common name comes from the fact that the plant was considered a species of aster for many years. Blossoms from the beginning of July to mid-August.

ASTER FLEABANE ⋎ **86**

Sunflower Family

Erigeron peregrinus

- Peregrine Fleabane, Wandering Daisy, Mountain Daisy

- Alaska south to California and New Mexico.

- Meadows and moist to semi-dry places on hillsides.

- Subalpine zone

Violet Family

Viola flettii

- Olympic Violet, Rock Violet
- Restricted to Olympic Mountains. Not in Cascades.
- Rock crevices and occasionally on talus slopes.
- Subalpine and Arctic-alpine zones

87 ↑ FLETT VIOLET

One must go into the high country of the Olympics to find this uncommon plant, particularly to the northern and eastern sections of the mountains. Compare it with Hook Violet (#91) with which it might be confused. The differences are so pronounced that the two can easily be separated. Note the large, flat, thick, kidney-shaped leaves of the Flett Violet as contrasted to the smaller, more oval leaves of the Hook Violet. The flowers differ, for the Flett Violet is not blue but a bluish-purple. It blossoms in late June and early July as soon as the snow melts from the warm south- and west-facing slopes. Look for it on Blue Mountain and in the Obstruction Point area.

Like all paintbrushes, the flowers are small and inconspicuous, hidden by the lavendar to magenta-colored bracts. The bracts are closely clustered at the upper part of an 8″ to 14″ stem, overlapping one another. Three varieties are recognized for northwestern Washington, and our variety, *olympica,* is confined to the Olympic Mountains. The other two varieties are similar to ours; *oreopola* in the Cascades south of Mt. Rainier, and *albida,* north of Mt. Rainier to southern British Columbia. Magenta Paintedcup blossoms from the end of June to the end of July. Common at Hurricane Ridge and along the road to Obstruction Point.

88 ↓ MAGENTA PAINTEDCUP

Figwort Family

Castilleja parviflora

- Magenta Paintbrush, Rosy Indian Paintbrush
- Southern Alaska south to Cascade and Olympic Mts., and Canadian Rockies.
- Open meadows where it is fairly moist and sunny.
- Subalpine zone

Waterleaf Family

Phacelia sericea

- Mt. Phacelia,
  Scorpionweed,
  Purple Fringe

- British Columbia south
  to northern California,
  east to Nevada and
  Colorado.

- Rocky, dry localities on
  sunny, open slopes.

- Subalpine and Arctic-
  alpine zones

SILKY PHACELIA ⋏ 89

The leaves are greyish-green, alternate, and are of a soft, silky texture because of the fine hairs that cover them. Well adapted to surviving in rather dry soil, Silky Phacelia tends to grow in clumps, and is 1' to 1½' tall. The flowers, massed on the top one-third of the stem, are light purple with long, conspicuous, purple stamens that have a yellow dot at the tip. The stamens extend from each flower to give a fuzzy appearance to the flower cluster. *Phacelia* is from *phacelus* (Gr.) a bundle or cluster, and *sericea* (Gr.) means silky. Blossoms from the end of June to the latter part of July.

The deep purple, irregular flowers are grouped at the top of a 1' to 2' stem. The petals are four, inconspicuously small, white, and hidden by the sepals that are petal-like. All parts of the plant are poisonous, especially the seeds. The juice of some delphiniums were used by Indians in dyeing baskets and other weaving material. *Delphinium* is probably from *delphi* (Gr.) a dolphin, because of the resemblance of the flower to a dolphin's head; *glareosum* is from *glareo* (L.) gravel, in reference to the rocky soil in which it is usually found. Blossoms from the beginning of July to the beginning of August.

LITTLE LARKSPUR ⅄ 90

Buttercup Family

Delphinium glareosum

- Gravel Larkspur

- Olympics and central
  Cascades of Washington
  and Oregon.

- Warm south- and east-
  facing slopes where soil
  is dry and rocky.

- Subalpine and Arctic-
  alpine zones

Violet Family

Viola adunca

- Western Dog Violet, Purple Violet, Blue Violet
- Widespread over most of temperate North America.
- Moist locations near streams, wet places, but more often in moist to dry meadows and hillsides.
- Montane Forest and Subalpine zones

91 ⋏ HOOK VIOLET

A short, 3″- to 4″-high, plant with deep blue, "pansy-like" flowers showing a white center. The flower is about ¾″ across and is of five petals, the lower petal the larger. Leaves are roundish to heart-shaped, finely toothed, long-stemmed, and mostly at the base of the plant. Some Indian groups thought the plant to be of some medicinal value; the roots and leaves were eaten at childbirth; the crushed flowers were used to relieve chest pains by placing them on the site of the pain. *Viola* is Latin for the color violet; *adunca* (L.) means hooked. Blossoms from the end of June to the beginning of August at its highest elevations.

A short plant, usually no more than 8″ high, that bears one- or two-massed whorls of small, ½″-long, bluish-purple flowers that often have a tinge of pink. The opposite, somewhat oval leaves seem matted for most of them are at the base of the plant. Three other penstemons are common in the park. The few-flowered Davidson's Penstemon, *P. davidsonii,* of rock crevices and talus slopes in the arctic-alpine zone; Eggleaf Penstemon, *P. ovatus,* of the subalpine zone; and Coast Penstemon, *P. serrulatus,* found from the lowland and humid lowland forest zones to the subalpine zone. Littleleaf Penstemon blossoms from the beginning of July to beginning of August.

92 ⋎ LITTLEFLOWER PENSTEMON

Figwort Family

Penstemon procerus

- Small-flowered Penstemon
- Alaska south to California and Colorado.
- Unusually warm, dry meadows or small, grassy vales in rocky areas.
- Arctic-alpine zone

Pea Family

Lathyrus nevadensis

- Wild Sweetpea
- British Columbia south to California, east to Idaho.
- Open forests and open hillsides among grasses.
- Upper Montane Forest zone and Subalpine zone

NUTTALL'S PEA ⋏ 93

The bluish-purple, sweetpea-like flowers of this plant are most often observed scattered over a subalpine hillside growing among the grasses. The flowers are usually paired, and number five or six per plant. The leaves are of paired leaflets, numbering about eight to ten pairs, and they are covered with very fine hairs. Nuttall's Pea is short and forms small clumps. It blossoms during July, and is fairly common on Hurricane Ridge and Blue Mountain.

Low growing, almost matted, this light blue to purplish-blue flowered plant is always found in cracks and crevices of rocks, so must be searched for in rocky outcroppings at high elevations. Petals are somewhat star-shaped and about 1″ across. Leaves are small with spiny margins. One of the most hardy of alpine plants, it is admirably suited to the harsh environment in which it is found. Its low form and small leaves permit it to conserve water and escape the affects of strong winds. *Campanula* is from *campan* (L.) a bell, and *piperi* is after C. V. Piper, an early-day Olympic Peninsula botanist. Blossoms from mid-July to August. A very uncommon pure white variety grows in scattered locations in the northeast portion of the mountains.

PIPER BELLFLOWER ⋎ 94

Bluebell Family

Campanula piperi

- Olympic Harebell
- Restricted to the Olympic Mts. Not in Cascades.
- Rock crevices that face south or southwest for maximum sun.
- Subalpine and Arctic-alpine zones

Figwort Family

Veronica cusickii

- Speedwell
- Olympic and Cascade Mts. south to northern Oregon, east to Idaho and Montana.
- Moist meadows, sunny hillsides.
- Subalpine and Arctic-alpine zones

95 ⋏ CUSICK SPEEDWELL

Sometimes almost hidden by meadow grasses and other plants, this pretty little wildflower bears a cluster of small, deep blue-purple flowers with yellow centers. The flowers crowd the upper part of a 2″ to 8″ erect stem. The leaves are opposite, elliptical to oval, and point upward. An uncommon white flowered form is sometimes observed mixed with the blue-purple plants. It is only a color variation, not a different plant. Blossoms from the end of June to the end of July. Common in meadows of Hurricane Hill.

A shrubby plant, 1′ to 3′ tall, with a mass of blue, sweetpea-like flowers on the upper part of each flowering stem. Each leaf is made up of seven to ten leaflets radiating out from a common point. Each plant can become covered with flowers at the peak of blossoming, to the extent of literally transforming a meadow into a sea of blue. The first flower buds begin to open about the middle of June, reaching the peak of its flowering period about the middle of July, and usually will be gone by the middle of August. *Lupinus* is from *lupin* (L.) wolf, because of the ability of plants of this genus to compete successfully with other plants. *Latifolis* is from *lati* (L.) broad or wide, and *folius* (L.) a leaf. Very common in the meadows of Hurricane Ridge.

96 ⋎ SUBALPINE LUPINE

Pea Family

Lupinus latifolius

- Broadleaf Lupine
- British Columbia south to California.
- Meadows and open forests where soil is not too moist.
- Subalpine zone

Bluebell Family

Campanula rotundifolia

- Bluebells of Scotland, Scotch Bluebell, Bellflower
- Northern regions of Europe, Asia, North America; south in mountains to northern California, New Mexico, and Texas.
- Meadows, roadsides where soil is dry.
- Subalpine and Arctic-alpine zones

AMERICAN HAREBELL ⋏ 97

Our American Harebell, more interestingly called the Bluebells of Scotland and immortalized by the Scottish poet Robert Burns, is common to the high elevations of the Olympics. The light blue, bell-shaped flowers brighten many roadsides, trailsides, and meadows. It is easily recognized despite the fact that different environments may cause it to grow differently; tall in rich soil with several flowers per stem, short with single flower per stem in dry situations at its highest elevation. *Rotund* (L.) for round and *folia* (L.) for a leaf, refers to the basal leaves which are rounded to somewhat heart-shaped. The stem leaves are alternate and narrow. Blossoms from mid-July to mid-August.

The most obvious characteristic of this polemonium is the pungent, skunk-like odor of the leaves, quite out of character for such a pretty plant. The light blue flowers have a tinge of pink at the center and are clustered at the ends of its stems. The leaves are of nine or more small, opposite leaflets that are light green. *Polemonium* is from *polemo* (Gr.) war, and *ium* (Gr.) small, for a plant of this kind is said by the great Roman naturalist, Pliny, to have led to war. *Pulcherrimum* is from *pulcher* (L.) which means beautiful. Blossoms from mid-June to as late as mid-August at the very high elevations.

SKUNKLEAF POLEMONIUM ⋎ 98

Phlox Family

Polemonium pulcherrimum

- Blue Skunkleaf, Jacob's Ladder, Showy Polemonium
- Alaska south to California, east to Colorado.
- Moist, shaded places; edge of tree clumps, near logs.
- Subalpine zone

Lily Family

Fritillaria lanceolata

- Purple Rice-bulbed Fritillary, Mission Bells, Checker Lily, Leopard Lily, Rice Root
- British Columbia south to southern California
- Grassy places near conifers
- Lowland, Humid Lowland Forest to Subalpine zone

99 ⋏ CHOCOLATE LILY

A lily whose nodding flowers consist of six brown mottled, greenish petals that form a cup. One to 2' tall, its narrow leaves form whorls about the upper part of the stem. The bulb is covered with white nodules that closely resemble rice. The bulb and nodules are edible. *Fritillaria* comes from *fritillus* (L.) a dice box, because of the resemblance of the flower markings to the companion of the dice box, the checker board. *Lanceolata* refers to the narrow form of the leaves. Blossoms during the month of July.

The flowers are often hidden from view for they form in the leaf axils close to the ground beneath the heart-shaped leaves. Brownish-purple, the flower lobes are spreading and tapering. The leaves are the more eye-catching part of the plant. The stem creeps over the ground with two leaves growing from each stem node. Tiny, white hairs can be seen on the veins and margins of the leaves as well as on the stems. The entire plant has a slight ginger odor, but is not related to the commercial ginger plant which is found in India and China. Of no medicinal qualities, although some Indians boiled it as a tonic tea. *Caudatum* is from *cauda* (L.) tail, referring to the tail-like appendages of the blossoms. In blossom from the end of June through July.

100 ⋎ BRITISH COLUMBIA WILDGINGER

Birthwort Family

Asarum caudatum

- Long-tailed Wild Ginger
- British Columbia south to central California, east in scattered locations to Idaho and Montana.
- Moist, partially shaded places in forests.
- Lowland Forest and Montane Forest zones